friendship bracelets
all grown up

friendship bracelets

all grown up

jo packham

Martingale®
& COMPANY

If you have any questions or comments, please contact:

Empire Road Productions
Jo Packham
215 Historic 25th Street
Ogden, Utah 84401
801-621-2777
www.empireroadproductions.com

Friendship Bracelets All Grown Up

Martingale & Company
20205 144th Ave. NE
Woodinville, WA 98072-8478 USA
www.martingale-pub.com

Credits

President & CEO	Tom Wierzbicki
Publisher	Jane Hamada
Editorial Director	Mary V. Green
Managing Editor	Tina Cook
Designer	Matt Shay
Photographer	Zac Williams
Copy Editor	Jenn Gibbs

Printed in China

13 12 11 10 09 08   8 7 6 5 4 3 2 1

Library of Congress Cataloging-in-Publication Data
Library of Congress Control Number: 2007017335

ISBN: 978-1-56477-846-8

Mission Statement
Dedicated to providing quality products and service to inspire creativity.

Once upon a time, Friendship Bracelets were a staple of summer camp and college roadtrips. They were shared between pals like packs of gum and autograph books, short-lived symbols of the easy alliances of youth. When the bracelet (or the friendship) showed too many signs of wear and tear, you'd simply snip the strings and let the bracelet go.

Now Friendship Bracelets are all grown up. Made from premium fibers and fancy beads, they're more like wearable art or expensive costume jewelry, yet they're just as fun and easy to make as the kid version. With just a handful of knots, you can create beautiful bracelets quickly, and they're still a pleasure to give and to get. The only difference is that, like your best adult friendships, these bracelets are real keepers.

In this book you'll find a wide range of inspiring project ideas that prove jewelry doesn't have to be complicated to be fabulous. Because necklaces are variations of the basic bracelet, I've included a few of these as well. (Some are even pieces from my personal collection.) They all show that, with a few techniques and some ingenuity, you can create chic, fun, elegant jewelry.

So, think young, gather those beautiful fibers, threads, and beads that you haven't known what to do with, and check out the following pages. It's time to get hip with the grown-up version of the Friendship Bracelet.

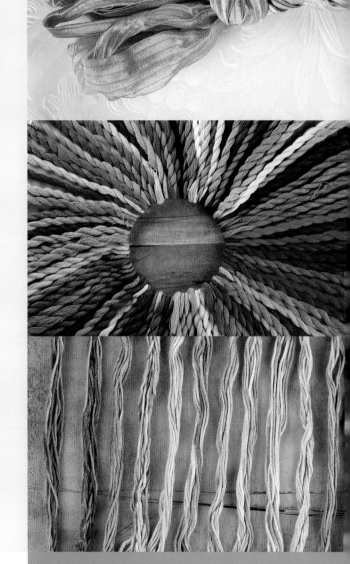

designer secret:

Friendship Bracelet techniques are so versatile, you can use them for making necklaces, chokers, ankle bracelets, bookmarks, zipper pulls, hair bands, embellishments for gifts—the list goes on.

table of contents

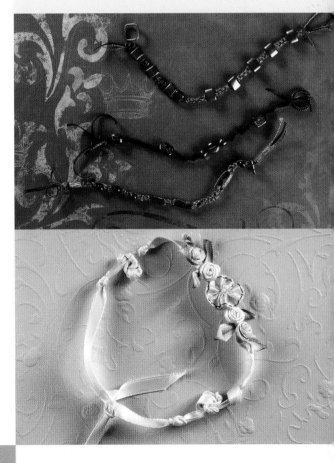

basic supplies

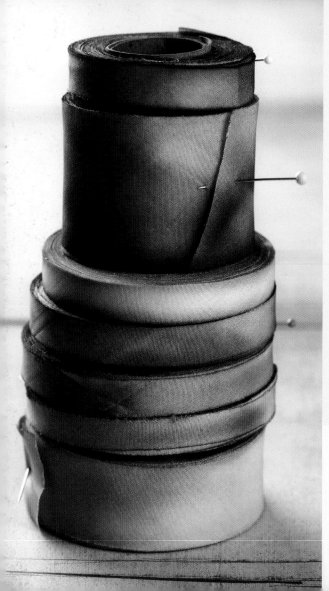

threads & strands

The trick to bringing your Friendship Bracelets into the designer zone is to upgrade your threads. A traditional Friendship Bracelet is made with **embroidery floss**, a relatively inexpensive material with a near-limitless color range and workability. Grown-up girls enhance this standard material with **novelty fibers** such as hand-dyed threads and satin or velvet ribbon. Sure, they're more of an investment, but they're cheaper than sterling silver—and they're gorgeous!

When selecting materials, keep an open mind and let creativity be your muse. Ribbon, rickrack, yarn, strands of silk, cotton fibers, wool, and even plain old string are all fair game. Basically, if you can knot it, you can use it (and if a knot slips, dab on a drop of fabric glue). As long as you combine elements and go beyond the everyday with your design, your bracelets will be spectacular.

A word on terms: because there's such an amazing variety of fibers you can use, this book uses the word **thread** unless referring to a specific type of fiber. You'll also see the word **strand** a lot. A strand may be any number of threads as long as you treat them as a single thread when you're working. For instance, you might use several threads of embroidery floss as one strand. Or you might combine one type of thread, such as ribbon, with another, like beaded wire, and use the combination as a single strand as you knot, braid, and so on. Thinking in terms of strands rather than just threads can make it easier to adapt a given pattern to whatever materials you feel inspired to use.

designer secret:

Are you a person who can't resist collecting beautiful materials like ribbons and beads even though you don't know what you'll do with them? Now's the time to pull them out!

knotting board & pins

A **Knotting Board** is a Friendship Bracelet necessity. It serves as a work surface, holding one end of the bracelet so you can focus on your work. The board should allow you to easily insert and remove pins yet be firm enough to hold them against gentle tugging. (Thick cardboard or foam core is perfect.) Extra-long **pins** (such as hatpins) are best for holding your knots to the board.

designer secret:

If you're making multiple bracelets, make a template by marking the lengths onto the board as you create the first one. Then you won't need to continually measure as you produce additional copies.

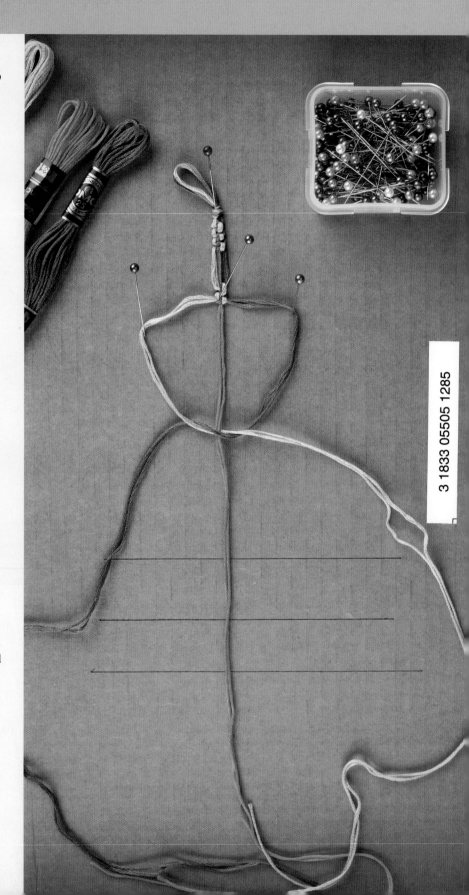

3 1833 05505 1285

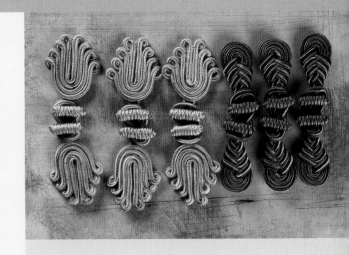

beads & other embellishments

Standout style depends on the unexpected touch, the delightful element of surprise. Look for beads and other embellishments that you truly love and your bracelets will reflect your passion. Beads can be any size and type—just notice whether the holes in them are a good size for the fibers you want to use. If they're too big, the bead may hang awkwardly off the thread, making the bracelet look sloppy. Too small, and you'll have to use an alternate method, such as a **Head Pin or Eye Pin**, to attach the bead.

To make it easier to string beads onto thread, try making your own **Beading Wire Loop** following the diagram *(see diagram)*. Insert the wire loop through the hole in a bead, slip one end of the thread through the loop, and pull the wire loop back through he bead to carry the thread through the hole.

You can also re-purpose vintage jewelry and other items such as unusual buttons and scrapbook embellishments to give your bracelet sophistication. Even **Chinese button closures** (also known as Chinese frogs) for sewing clothes can be used as decorative clasps. If a finding is the right size and delights you thoroughly, it has the potential to become part of an inspired piece of jewelry.

beading wire loop

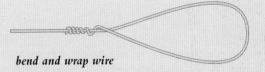

bend and wrap wire

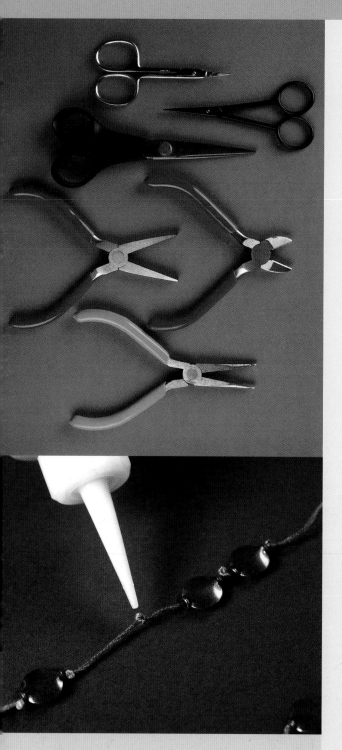

scissors & jewelry tools

Designer results depend on attention to detail, including clean, precise cuts just where you want them. You'll need very small scissors with narrow points (called **snips**) for clipping fine threads close to the clasps and medium-sized **shears** for general clipping. Both pairs of scissors should be kept in top working condition by being used only on fabric and fiber—never on anything else.

You should also have a pair of **needle-nose pliers** and jeweler's **wire cutters** on hand for projects that call for traditional beading and wire techniques. In a pinch, a pair of sturdy, all-purpose scissors can be substituted for the wire cutters, but if you're serious about making bracelets, it's worth it to get the right tool for the job. Ordinary **tweezers** can also come in handy for pulling threads through small openings, undoing accidental knots, and more.

adhesives

You may sometimes need to secure your fibers with a touch of adhesive. For the best results, choose one that is permanent, dries invisible, and is pliable. Before you add the adhesive to your piece, test it on a sample strand of the fiber you're using to make sure it won't discolor or otherwise distort the material. When applying adhesive to the bracelet, keep in mind that a little goes a long way. Using a fine-tipped applicator or a pin can help you control the glue more precisely.

If you want to adhere beads and other embellishments to your design, make sure the adhesive you use is suitable for both the embellishment and the section of bracelet you want it to stick to. For example, fabric glue may not hold a plastic button to a fiber base as well as an all-purpose craft glue. Most fabric and craft shops offer a variety of adhesives that are labeled with guidelines for use.

wire

Many Friendship Bracelet patterns call for a piece of wire for adding beads and other elements. **Jewelry wire** comes in different gauges (diameters). The higher the gauge, the thinner the wire. You may need to experiment to find the perfect wire for a project. If you use a wire that's too thick, it could be unworkable or look amateurish. On the other hand, if it's too thin it may break when the bracelet is worn.

Jewelry wire is available in gold, copper, silver, and a variety of both metallic and coated colors. Color matters if your beads are transparent; otherwise, the wire will probably be concealed.

jump rings

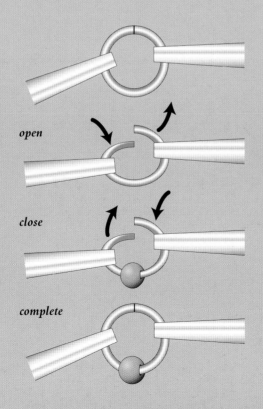

open

close

complete

jump rings

Jump rings are small circles that you can use to attach an embellishment or clasp to your bracelet. Use two pairs of pliers, or tweezers, to pull the jump ring open. Slip each of the items being joined onto the jump ring, and then squeeze it closed. *(see diagram)*

wire wrapping

wrapping with same wire–head pin example

Fig. 1

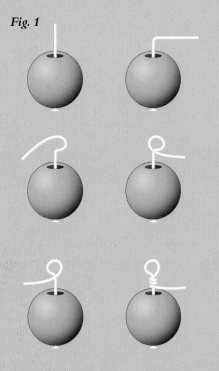

wrapping with separate wire–eye pin example

Fig. 2

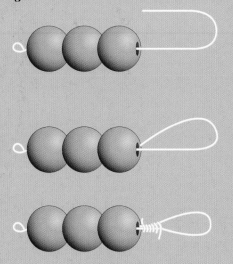

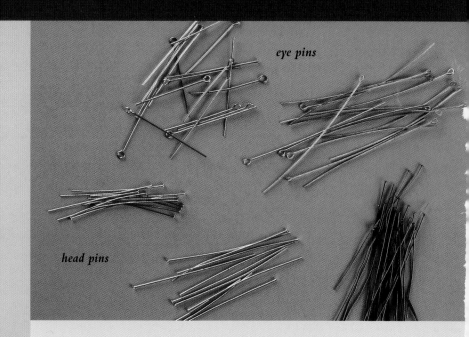

eye pins

head pins

head pins and eye pins

Head pins look a bit like straight pins for sewing, but they're made for jewelry and sometimes have very decorative tops (heads). **Eye pins** have a loop at the top. Both range from almost 1" to 4" long and are available in gold, silver, bronze, and copper with different gauge wire stems, and they're great for creating dangles on Friendship Bracelets.

Wire wrapping is a technique used to fasten head pins and eye pins to your jewelry piece. You can wrap a pin with its own stem or with a separate piece of wire.

materials

head pin or eye pin, beads, needle-nose pliers or tweezers

instructions:

1. Use pliers to straighten the pin's stem if necessary.

2. Slide beads onto the stem. Bend the stem and form a loop. Wrap the excess wire around the stem at the base of the loop. *Fig. 1* Alternatively, you can wrap and secure the loop with a separate piece of wire. *Fig. 2*

(Note: Wrapping with the same wire or a separate wire can be used with either head pins or eye pins.)

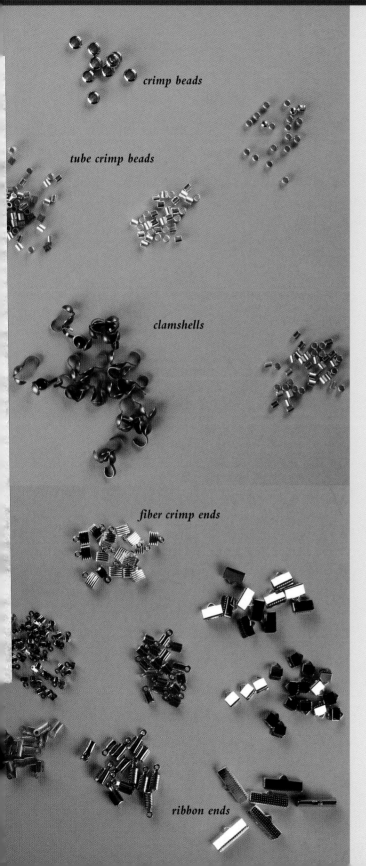

crimp beads

tube crimp beads

clamshells

fiber crimp ends

ribbon ends

crimp beads

Many projects in this book call for working with wire. To finish the ends of wires, you can thread them into **round crimp beads** and press them closed with ordinary needle–nosed pliers. **Tube crimp beads** are also used for wire. They look more professional but require special crimping pliers that come in different sizes for working with different sizes of tube crimps.

materials

crimp bead, clasp, jewelry wire, pliers (needle-nose or crimping)

instructions:

1. Thread a crimp bead onto the wire leaving one short end. Now thread a clasp onto the wire.

2. Thread the short end of the wire back through the crimp bead, creating a loop. (Note: The clasp is at the end of the loop.)

3. Hold the wire and slide the crimp bead against the base of the clasp.

4. Place the crimp bead in the back of the pliers' jaws and squeeze the pliers shut. (Note: If using tube crimp beads, be sure to use the correct size of crimping pliers and follow the manufacturer's directions.)

special crimps

Some crimp beads are designed for use with fibers rather than wire. **Clamshells** close over the ends of smaller threads while **fiber crimp ends** and **ribbon ends** are made for wider, thicker fibers.

materials

clamshell or ribbon end, fibers, glue, pliers, snips

instructions:

1. Knot your strands and place the knot inside the clamshell or ribbon end. Apply a drop of adhesive to the knot and let it dry.

2. Trim excess threads and use pliers to close the clamshell or ribbon end.

15

bead cones

Finishing the ends of your Friendship Bracelets with **bead cones** will make them much more professional-looking. Bead cones let you hide loose threads inside them. Some bead cones are quite fancy, made of filigreed metal, decorated ceramic, and other materials, while others are simple and inexpensive.

materials

bead cone, bracelet, jewelry wire or glue, jump ring or clasp

instructions:

Option 1:

1. Use wire to wrap the loose ends of your knotted bracelet.
2. Push the wrapped threads into the bead cone and thread the end of the wire through the bead cone hole.
3. Attach the wire to a jump ring or clasp.

Option 2:

1. Glue together all but one of the loose fiber ends of your knotted bracelet.
2. Push the glued fibers into your bead cone and thread the single loose fiber through the bead cone hole.
3. Tie the single loose fiber to a jump ring or clasp.

clasps

Clasps are a key difference between traditional Friendship Bracelets and the grown-up variety. They connect the ends of a bracelet so you can take it off and put it on without damaging it. Some clasps are simple and subtle while others are works of art in themselves and act as embellishments to your design. There are even multi-strand clasps that can turn several bracelets into one. Just make sure whatever clasp you choose is the right color, size, and shape for your project and is secure enough to hold the bracelet closed.

a word about length

Determining the length of threads, novelty fibers, and wire for your Friendship Bracelets is far from an exact science. The width of the fibers, number of strands, type of closure, and techniques you use—wrapping, weaving, and knotting—all affect the length you'll need. If you add beads or other embellishments into the mix, you'll need even longer strands.

Working with very long fibers can be difficult; having to stop and untangle threads every few minutes can take some of the fun out of a project. For projects that require extra-long threads, consider working with relatively short threads at first, tying on extensions to the individual threads as needed. If the knots can't be hidden in the wrapping, weaving, or knotting, consider covering them with an embellishment or simply make them a part of the design. Another solution is to work the entire piece in short sections, then knot or stitch the sections together.

tips for gauging length

- For a bracelet whose threads are going to be tied together at the end and that has simple knots or just a few complicated knots, you should use three times the length of the finished bracelet plus add 2-3" for ending. If you are going to fold the measured threads in half, then you should use six times the length.

- If your bracelet will be made with all Wrapping, Overhand Knots, Square Knots, Chevrons, or Diagonal Stripe Pattern in embroidery floss, start with strands that are four times as long as the finished bracelet, plus a bit extra for ending. If you're going to fold the threads in half, then you should use eight times the length.

- The thicker the fiber, the longer your threads will have to be.

- The more threads you have in a strand, the longer your threads will have to be.

- Typically, bracelets come in 7", 8", and 9" lengths, and ankle bracelets are between 9" and 12".

wraps

basic wrapping

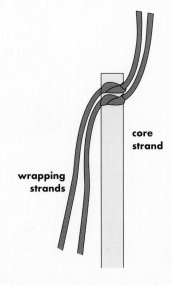

core strand

wrapping strands

wrapping with alternating colors

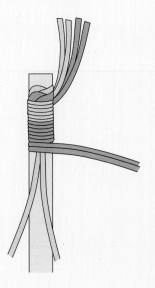

basic wrapping

materials

core strand, wrapping strands

instructions:

1. Cut the core strand to be the length of the finished bracelet plus extra for tying or attaching a clasp. Cut two wrapping strands four times the length of the core thread. Tie the wrapping strands to the core strand. *(see diagram)*

2. Pin the knotted end of your project to the Knotting Board. Tightly wrap both wrapping strands around the core strand until you get to the end. Knot the end. (Note: You can do this technique with just one wrapping strand if you double its length.)

wrapping with alternating colors

materials

core strand, 2 different colors of wrapping strands

instructions:

1. Cut the core strand to the desired length of the finished bracelet plus extra for finishing. Cut at least two wrapping strands of different colors. Each should be eight times the length of the core thread. Fold the wrapping strands in half and cut in two to create your wrapping strands. Tie to the core strand at one end.

2. Pin the core strand to the Knotting Board. Hold one color of wrapping strands to the core strand. Wrap the other color of wrapping strands around both the first wrapping strands and the core strand so that only one color shows on the outside.

3. When you're ready to switch colors, hold the first wrapping strands to the core strand and wrap both the first wrapping strands and the core strand with the second color. *(see diagram)* Continue, alternating colors as desired.

4. When you reach the end of the core strand, tie all the strands together in a tight knot to finish. (Note: You can do this technique with more than two colors of wrapping strands to create a multicolored striped bracelet.)

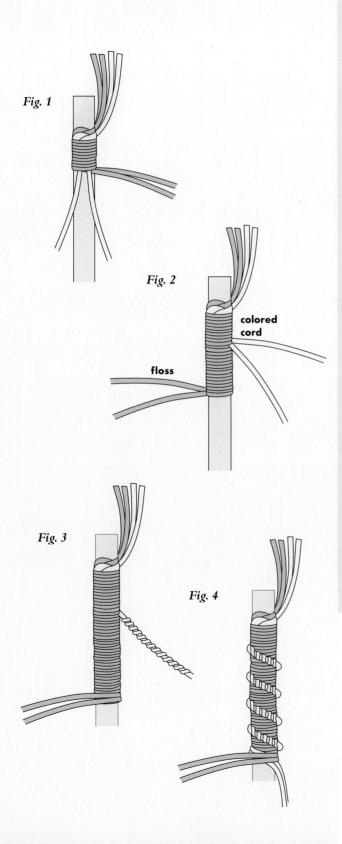

Fig. 1

Fig. 2

colored
cord

floss

Fig. 3

Fig. 4

double-wrapping
with cord

materials

core strand, embroidery floss, cord

instructions:

1. Cut a core strand the length of the bracelet plus extra for finishing. Cut a wrapping strand of floss eight times as long as the core strand. Cut a length of cord four times as long as the core strand.

2. Fold the wrapping strand in half, cut it in two, and tie one end of the two wrapping strands to one end of the core strand. Repeat this step with the cord.

3. Pin the core strand to the Knotting Board. Wrap the two wrapping strands around the core strand and the two cords for about ½". *Fig. 1*

4. Pull the two cords away from the core and place them out of the way. Continue to wrap the core strand with the wrapping strands to the end. *Fig. 2*

5. Twist the two cords around each other to the ends of the cords then wrap the twisted cords around the wrapped core. *Fig. 3*

6. Wrap wrapping strands over cords and tie both in a knot. *Fig. 4*

designer secret:

A core strand can be just one or two threads or many. Just keep in mind that the thicker the core strand, the longer your wrapping strands will need to be. (Note too that slippery fibers such as silk cord don't make ideal core strands as they may not hold a wrap very well.)

twist & shout

materials

threads (28" lengths of as many strands as desired)

instructions:

1. Knot one end of all the strands together, leaving a long enough tail to finish the bracelet. Pin the knot to your Knotting Board. *Fig. 1*

2. Holding the loose ends of the strands together, twist them several times until they are very tight. *Fig. 2*

3. Pull the twisted strands straight and place your finger in the center of the twisted length. Fold the twisted strands in half and remove your finger. *Fig. 3*

4. Double-knot the loose end around the existing knot. (Note: If you can't hide the knot you tied in step 1 with this new knot, you can trim it off or untie it.) Remove the project from your Knotting Board. You can finish by threading the double-knot through the loop on the opposite end and tying it, or by crimping the loose end, attaching a clasp, then attaching a jump ring and clasp to the looped end. *Fig. 4*

Fig. 1

Fig. 2

Fig. 3

Fig. 4

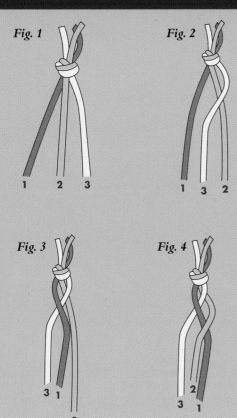

Fig. 1

1   2   3

Fig. 2

1   3   2

Fig. 3

3 1

2

Fig. 4

2
3   1

braiding

materials

threads (3 strands in 3 colors)

instructions:

1. Measure three strands three times the length of the bracelet, plus extra for finishing.

2. Knot the strands together about 1" from the top. Pin the knot to your Knotting Board and separate the strands. *Fig. 1*

3. Cross the far right strand over the middle strand. *Fig. 2*

4. Cross the far left strand over the middle strand. *Fig. 3*

5. Continue braiding bracelet by repeating from step 3. *Fig. 4*

1-2-3 weaving

materials

threads (3 strands in 3 colors)

instructions:

1. Cut two strands of two colors of thread two times the length of the finished bracelet and one strand of the third color of thread six times the length of the finished bracelet, plus extra for finishing. Knot the strands together about 1" from the top. Pin the knot to the Knotting Board and separate the strands so that the longer strand is on the right as strand #3. *Fig. 1*

2. Holding strands #1 and #2 straight and tight, weave strand #3 over strand #2 and under strand #1. Then weave back over strand #1 and under strand #2. *Fig. 2*

3. Slide weaving up towards the top knot so that it covers strands #1 and #2 completely. Continue weaving to the end of the strands. *Fig. 3*

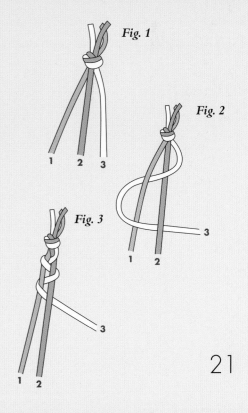

Fig. 1

1   2   3

Fig. 2

1   2

3

Fig. 3

1   2

3

1   2

21

4-strand weave

materials

threads (4 strands in 2 colors)

instructions:

1. Cut two lengths of each color thread (for four strands total) eight times the length of the finished bracelet, plus extra for finishing. Fold the lengths in half and tie a knot about 1" from the looped end. Now you have eight strands. Pin the knot to your Knotting Board, and separate the strands so that four strands of one color are on the right and four strands of the other color are on the left. ***Fig. 1***

2. Take the far right pair of strands (Group #4) under the pair of strands next to them (Group #3) and under the next pair (Group #2). Bring Group #4 strands back over Group #2 and leave them in the middle. ***Fig. 2***

3. Take the far left pair of strands (Group #1) under the strands next to them (Group #2), as well as under Group #4. Bring Group #1 back over Group #4 and leave them in the middle. Pull the groups tightly to the top. ***Fig. 3***

4. Repeat steps 2 and 3. (Note: The group numbers will change to reflect the position of the strands at the start of each new segment.) Continue for the desired length of the bracelet.

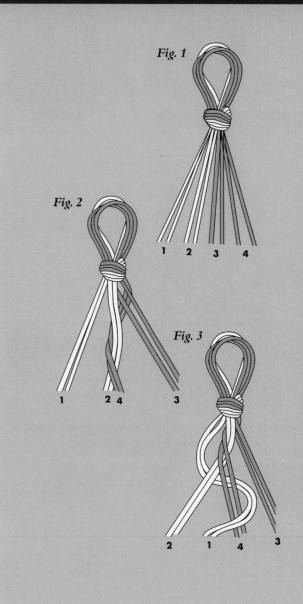

designer secret:

Thanks to the nature of fibers, techniques such as twisting, braiding, and weaving make Friendship Bracelets unlike any other kind of jewelry.

helpful hints for
weaving & knotting

- Knots are the heart and soul of a Friendship Bracelet. If you're at all intimidated by learning knots, start with a design that uses just one or two. In no time at all, you'll be ready for more!

- Choose thread that's the right thickness for your project. The finer the thread, the longer your bracelet will take to create and the more delicate it will seem. Thicker threads take a lot less time to work with and result in chunkier jewelry.

- While some designs look better when your weaves or knots are consistent, you might like the texture you get when you vary the tightness.

- To avoid confusion when working with multiple colors of thread, jot down the order in which they are used and pin the list to your knotting board.

- At first you might find yourself forgetting the exact steps to create a particular knot. If this happens but you like what you have created instead, keep it! There isn't really a right or wrong way to knot—there's only what you like.

designer secret:

If your bracelet starts to twist as you work, pin the knots to your knotting board as you go. When you have enough knots in a row for the bracelet to be twisted around completely at least once, unpin the knots, twist the bracelet, pin the twisted part to the board, and resume knotting.

right overhand knot

Fig. 1   **Fig. 2**

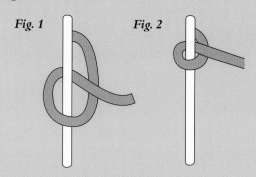

Fig. 3   **Fig. 4**

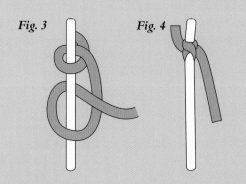

left overhand knot

Fig. 5   **Fig. 6**

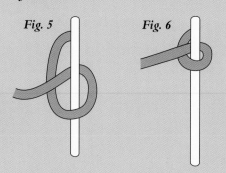

Fig. 7   **Fig. 8**

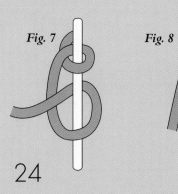

overhand knots

You can make Overhand Knots with as many threads as you please. Unless otherwise specified, you can make either a Right Overhand Knot or a Left Overhand Knot for any project that calls for an Overhand Knot. Note that a series of Right or Left Overhand Knots results in a pretty spiral effect.

materials

threads (2 or more strands)

instructions:

Option 1: right overhand knot

1. Cut at least two strands to be four times the length of the finished bracelet, plus extra for finishing. (Double the length if you'll be folding the threads in half before you start knotting.)

2. Tightly hold the left-hand strand straight and loop the remaining strand around it as shown. *Fig.1*

3. Pull the working strand to the right until tight. (Stop here for a half Overhand Knot.) *Fig. 2*

4. Repeat steps 2 and 3, inserting the end through the loop as shown. *Fig. 3*

5. Finished Right Overhand Knot. *Fig. 4*

Option 2: left overhand knot

1. Cut at least two strands to be four times the length of the finished bracelet, plus extra for finishing. (Double the length if you'll be folding the threads in half before you start knotting.)

2. Tightly hold the right-hand strand straight and loop the remaining strand around it as shown. *Fig. 5*

3. Pull the working strand to the left until tight. (Stop here for a half Overhand Knot) *Fig. 6*

4. Repeat steps 2 and 3, inserting the end through the loop as shown. *Fig. 7*

5. Finished Left Overhand Knot. *Fig. 8*

basic diagonal stripe

materials

threads (4 different colors), clasp

instructions:

1. Cut one strand of each color thread (for four strands total) four times the desired length of the finished bracelet, plus extra for finishing. Tie a knot about 1" from the top and pin it to your Knotting Board. *Fig. 1*

2. Separate the strands. *Fig. 2*

3. Beginning on the far left, tie strand #1 in an Overhand Knot over strand #2. *Fig. 3*

4. Continuing with strand #1, tie an Overhand Knot around each of the remaining strands. *Fig. 4*

5. Strand #2 should now be on the far left. Begin the process again, tying Overhand Knots with strand #2 over strands #3, #4, and #1. *Fig. 5*

6. Repeat steps 3-5. (Note: The strand numbers will change to reflect the position of the strands at the start of each new segment.) Continue for the desired length of the bracelet. *Fig. 6*

designer secret:

The basic patterns for Friendship Bracelets—a Diagonal Stripe and a Chevron—are easier to learn with embroidery floss. To make these patterns look professional, make your knots nice and even by pulling each one to the same degree of tightness. This technique will be more challenging to master when you add other fibers to your designs.

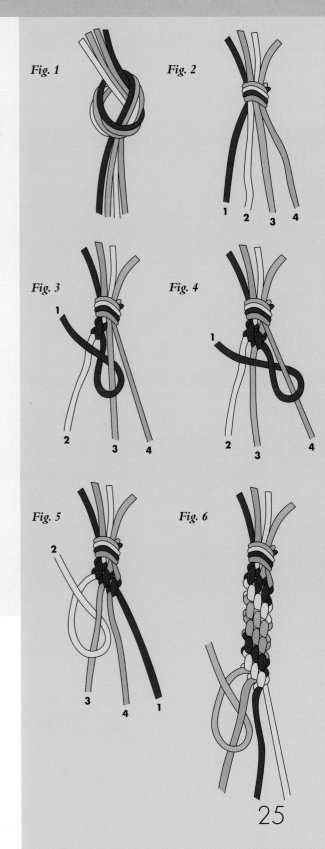

Fig. 1 Fig. 2 Fig. 3 Fig. 4 Fig. 5 Fig. 6

25

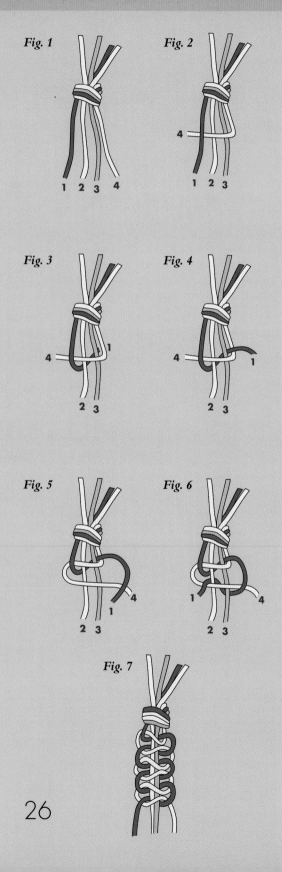

Fig. 1

Fig. 2

Fig. 3

Fig. 4

Fig. 5

Fig. 6

Fig. 7

square knots

The following instructions for Square Knots and Square Knots with Picots call for four strands, but you can make them with three strands too. Just treat the middle strand as though it's the same as the #2 and #3 strands.

materials

threads (4 strands in 4 colors)

instructions:

1. Cut each of the four strands to be four times the desired length of the finished bracelet, plus extra for finishing. Knot the strands together at one end and pin the knot to the Knotting Board. Separate the strands. **Fig. 1**

2. Move strand #4 from the far right and cross it over the center strands (#2 and #3) and under strand #1. **Fig. 2**

3. Move strand #1 behind strands #2 and #3 and through the loop in strand #4 (far right). **Fig. 3 & Fig. 4**

4. Pull on strands #1 and #4 to create the first half of the Square Knot.

5. Move strand #4 from the left and cross it over the center strands (#2 and #3) and under strand #1. **Fig. 5**

6. Bring strand #1 under strands #2 and #3 and through the loop on the left. **Fig. 6**

7. Pull on strands #1 and #4 to finish the Square Knot.

8. Repeat steps 2–8 to desired length. **Fig. 7**

designer secret:

While this pattern is easier to create when you use multiple colors, a single hue can show off the great texture.

square knot with raised picots

This easy design uses raised picots—small loops of thread—between sets of Square Knots to create extra texture and interest. While these instructions call for six knots on either side of a raised picot, you can vary the number as desired.

materials

threads (4 strands)

instructions:

1. Follow the instructions for creating a Square Knot (Making the Square Knots tight will make picots more visible). Repeat until you have six Square Knots.

2. After every sixth knot, leave a very small extra space, then make six more Square Knots. *Fig.1*

3. To create the Raised Picot, pull the two center strands up and through the space between the sets of Square Knots. Pull tight. *Fig. 2* (Note: You may use a crochet hook if the threads are difficult to pull through.)

4. Bring the strands back to position. Repeat the pattern (six Square Knots, a small space, six more Square Knots, a Raised Picot) until the bracelet is the desired length.

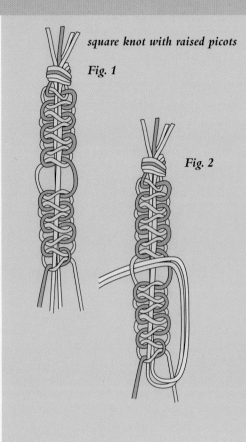

square knot with raised picots

Fig. 1

Fig. 2

placement knot

Use this technique when you need to make a knot in a specific place, such as right next to a bead.

instructions:

1. Tie one Overhand Knot, but do not pull it tight. *Fig. 1*

2. While holding the bracelet thread with one hand, use the other hand to place the tips of your tweezers through the knot. Squeeze the tweezers at the point where you want the knot to be. *Fig. 2*

3. While holding the tweezers, pull the threads to tighten the knot. *Fig. 3*

4. Place the smallest possible drop of adhesive on the knot.

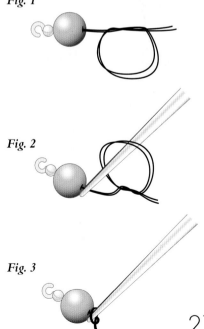

placement knot

Fig. 1

Fig. 2

Fig. 3

27

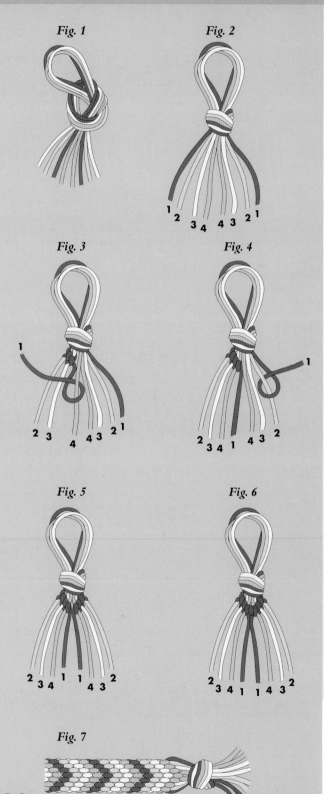

Fig. 1

Fig. 2

Fig. 3

Fig. 4

Fig. 5

Fig. 6

Fig. 7

chevron

materials

threads (4 different colors)

instructions:

1. Cut one strand of each color (for four strands total) to be eight times the desired length of the finished bracelet, plus extra for finishing. Fold the four strands in half, tie a knot 1" from the looped end, and pin the knot to the Knotting Board. *Fig. 1*

2. Separate the strands and arrange them so the colors mirror each other. *Fig. 2*

3. Take strand #1 from the far left and make one Left Overhand Knot onto strand #2. Repeat with strand #3 then #4, working toward the center. Stop knotting and leave strand #1 in the center. *Fig. 3*

4. Take strand #1 from the far right and, working to the center, make one Right Overhand Knot onto strand #2, then #3, then #4. *Fig. 4*

5. Knot strands #1 and #1 together using an Overhand Knot. (Note: You can use either a Left or Right Overhand Knot for this step—just use the same type each time you perform this step so the center knots will all go the same direction.) *Fig. 5 & Fig. 6*

6. Beginning with the outermost strands and working toward the center, repeat as in steps 3–5 until you reach the desired length.

7. Knot the ends together to finish. *Fig. 7*

The projects in this book may be finished in any number of ways—it all depends on what you like. Mix and match different techniques to design your own unique jewelry!

loose ends

Sometimes, leaving the ends loose isn't just the simplest method of ending your bracelet—it's a pretty one, too.

Option 1:

When the bracelet has loose strands at both ends, simply wrap it around the wrist and tie the ends in a double knot. Trim the loose ends to the desired length. *Fig.1* Simply knotting a ribbon bracelet can make the loose ends an important part of the design. *Fig. 2*

Option 2:

Knot one end of your bracelet, thread the loose end or ends through an embroidery needle, and weave it back into the body of the bracelet. *Fig. 3*

Option 3:

To add a designer touch to a loose ends bracelet, stitch a covered hook-and-eye to the underside of each end. *Fig. 4*

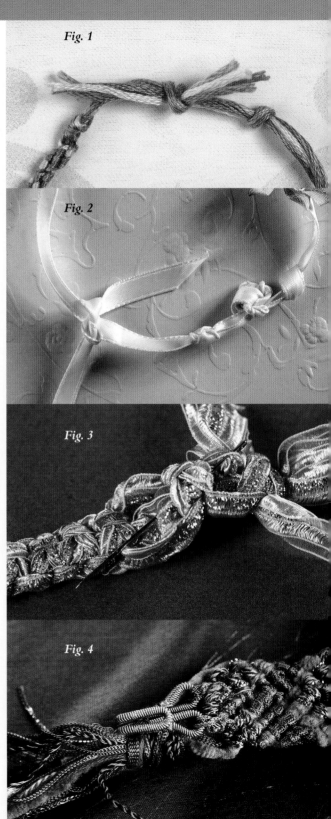

Fig. 1

Fig. 2

Fig. 3

Fig. 4

Fig. 1

looped ends

Folding the threads in half when starting the bracelet will create a loop at one end that can be used as part of a closure.

Option 1:

Wrap the finished bracelet around your wrist, divide the threads at the loose end in half, and slip one half of the threads through the loop. *Fig. 1* Tie to the other half of the threads, securing them in a double knot.

Fig. 2

Option 2:

For a stylish finish on a looped-end bracelet, stitch a button to the straight end. Make sure it's just the right size to slip through the loop on the opposite end and hold fast. *Fig. 2*

Fig. 3

Option 3:

This is a sophisticated closure that allows the wearer to adjust the bracelet's fit. The alternating rings are actually wrapped pieces of elastic so that the bead attached to the loop on the opposite end can be inserted into any of the elastic loops. *Fig. 3*

jewelry clasps

Adding a clasp to the ends of your bracelet makes it possible for the piece to be taken on and off more easily and can make the piece appear more sophisticated overall. Clasps are easiest to attach when you use strands that are equivalent in strength to a minimum of three embroidery floss threads.

Option 1:

Using fiber crimp beads at the ends of your knotting makes it easy to attach a professional-looking clasp. *Fig. 1*

Option 2:

Combining a fiber tube with a popular style of clasp can make a bracelet look polished and pretty. *Fig. 2*

special knotted closure

This closure allows the bracelet to be tightened and loosened. Using a separate piece of cord, create a series of Square Knots over the two bracelet ends. *Fig. 3*

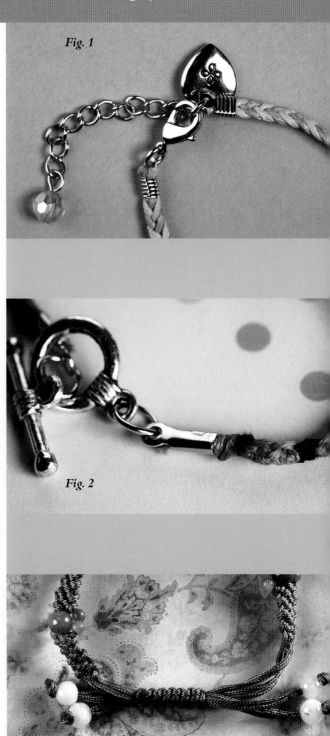

Fig. 1

Fig. 2

Fig. 3

31

lavender pansy

This pretty floral-themed necklace was made with lavender rattail cord, variegated lavender embroidery floss, and a porcelain flower and buds. To create, braid the floss for 2", tie two Square Knots, then repeat. Tie the braided floss and rattail together in a loose knot towards the end of the necklace. Attach a porcelain flower to the center and a bud to each end.

with all my heart

This piece mainly uses one color of thread woven in a Diagonal Stripe Pattern with beads and buttons added at random.

From a private collection.

instructions:

1. Create three groups of three floss strands each (one strand of each color in each group). Use 1-2-3 Weaving to weave each separate group, using a different color for Strand #3 (the weaving strand).

2. Attach fiber crimp beads to the ends of the fiber strands.

3. String plain beads onto wire and attach wire crimps to each end of the wire.

4. Slide bunny beads onto head pins accented with seed beeds, and wrap the stems of the pins around themselves. Use small jump rings to attach the wrapped head pins to one of the woven strands.

5. Attach each end of the four strands to a large jump ring. Attach a clasp to finish.

materials

embroidery floss (3 colors), crimp beads for wire & fiber, glass bunny beads, head pins, jewelery wire, large jump ring, plain beads (two colors), small jump rings

dream

Though the braiding technique used for this bracelet is simple, the overall effect is more sophisticated than a traditional braided Friendship Bracelet, thanks to how beautifully it's been finished.

From a private collection.

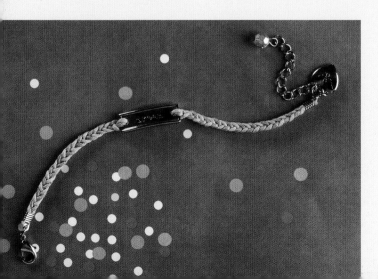

sleek-as-silk bracelet

Created by wrapping silk strands around a core strand, this elegant bracelet shows off the maker's skill.

From a private collection.

sleek-as-silk necklaces

The designer created these necklaces by wrapping and knotting cords and then adding pendants.

From a private collection.

instructions:

1. Cut two strands of ribbon and thread them through the loop in one half of the Chinese button closure. Fold the ribbons in half with the closure at the top of the loop.

2. Tie the two ribbons together using a series of Square Knots. Continue for the length of the bracelet (minus the closure).

3. Thread the end of the knotted ribbon through a loop in the other half of the closure. Wrap the tail of the ribbon around the joint, then use a needle to thread the ribbon back through the knots.

materials

¼" **ribbon**, Chinese button closure, large-eyed needle

what time is it?

This watchband can be made in minutes, literally. The textures of the novelty threads make the project appear much more complicated than it actually is. Simply loop the threads through the loops on the watch and tie the strands with Square Knots—that's it!

35

flower girl

For this bracelet, a wire wrapped with the stems of silk and paper flowers is combined with novelty fibers tied with Square Knots. The result is a piece that can be worn equally well with jeans or to a wedding.

daisy chain

A matching necklace is easy to create using the same materials and techniques as the bracelet above; just increase the strand lengths and, if desired, the number of embellishments.

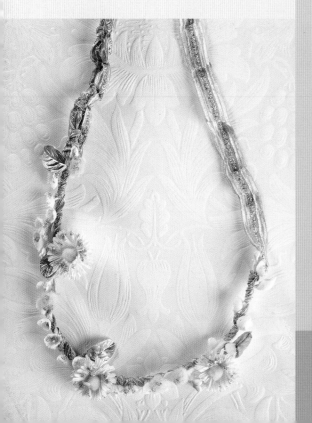

instructions:

1. Cut two strands of floss and one length of wire eight times the length of the finished bracelet, plus extra for finishing. Fold them in half and tie a knot 1" from the fold. String beads onto the wire and attach a crimp bead at the end.

2. Use the 4-Strand Weave technique, including the beaded wire with one of the floss strands. (Note: It doesn't matter which strand the wire is joined with, but do keep the wire with the same strand as you weave.) Weave until you reach the desired length then knot the loose end.

3. Stitch the button to the middle of the bracelet using needle and thread.

materials

embroidery floss (2 colors), beads, crimp bead, decorative glass button, jewelry wire, needle and thread

peek-a-bead necklace

For a fresh take on a jewelry set, make a necklace that matches the bracelet, but change the embellishment for added interest.

bolo necklace

A beaded bolo tie finds its perfect complement: delicate thread tied in Overhand Knots with beads added periodically.

From a private collection.

chocolate twist

Unusual fiber jewelry tubes and a matching clasp make this Twist & Shout bracelet unique.

From a private collection.

Silver bangles are transformed by fibers tied around the bracelets with Overhand Knots or wrapped with beaded wire. To finish the bracelet, use a sewing needle to weave the ends of the fibers back into the knots.

This silver bracelet is wrapped with beaded wire.

materials

embroidery floss (3 colors), jewelry wire, jump rings, miniature rickrack, multi-strand clasp, tube crimp beads, various beads (black glass, fimo clay disks, glass flowers, glass penguins, plastic disks, and yellow glass)

penguin pride

instructions:

1. Alternate jump rings with clay and plastic disks.

2. String penguin and flower beads onto wire and finish both ends with tube crimp beads.

3. Repeat step 2 with yellow and black beads.

4. Crimp one strand of each color of embroidery floss together, and tie four Square Knots. Switch the outside knotting threads and make four Square Knots. Switch the outside knotting threads again and make four square knots. Repeat the knot pattern down the length of the bracelet and crimp the end.

5. Cut the rickrack to the length of the bracelet and attach fiber crimps to each end.

6. Use jump rings to attach all five pieces to a multi-strand clasp to finish.

instructions:

1. Attach beads to the gold chain with head pins and/or jump rings.

2. Attach clasps to either end of the chain.

3. Using four strands of embroidery floss, tie a series of Square Knots half the length of the bracelet chain.

4. Create one Raised Picot.

5. Tie Square Knots for the rest of the knotted strand.

6. Knot one end of the knotted strand to the end of the embellished chain. Dab with glue.

7. Weave the knotted strand through the bracelet chain. Knot the other end to the end of your bracelet and dab with glue. Weave the loose ends back into the bracelet to finish.

materials

embroidery floss, clasp, crimp tubes, glue, gold chain, head pins, jump rings, various beads (birds, disks, and rings)

just ducky

This bracelet is created with glass beads strung on wire, a small glass duck on a head pin, and black embroidery floss tied in Square Knots with Picots. Jump rings connect each end of the strands to the clasp.

materials

cord, **variegated embroidery floss**, beads, clasp, jewelry wire, medallion, tassels

instructions:

1. Tie the cord onto the medallion and add a bead.

2. String beads onto wire.

3. Using one strand of embroidery floss for the core strand and one strand of embroidery floss for knotting, tie Overhand Knots.

4. Tie the beaded wire to the knotted floss and add a dab of glue to the knot. When dry, slide the bead up the medallion cord and knot the wire-and-floss strand to the cord. Slide the bead down to hide the knot.

5. Tie tassels to the bottom of the medallion and add a clasp to finish.

lost and found

Have a favorite earring that's lost its mate? Turn it into a pendant! Create a beaded "chain" with beading thread and beads. String small groups of beads onto the thread and tie Overhand Knots on both sides of each grouping to keep the beads in place. Attach the earring pendant with a jump ring.

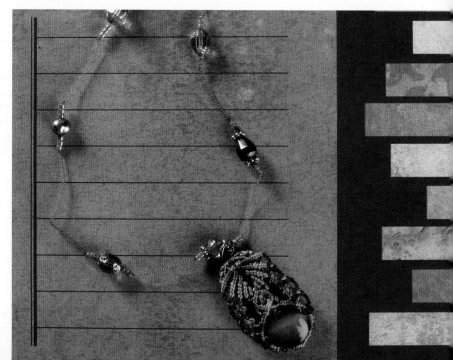

This cheery bracelet starts with a Basic Diagonal Stripe bracelet made with five colors of embroidery floss. Use jump rings to attach playful charms to the knotted strands.

here, kitty

An ordinary silver chain is woven with knotted and beaded strands, then embellished further with playful beads.

43

carmen miranda's bracelet

materials

¼" **ribbon**, glass button (sized to act as a clasp), glass fruit and vegetable beads, needle and thread

instructions:

1. Cut a length of ribbon twice as long as the finished bracelet, plus extra for finishing. Fold it in half. Leaving a loop on the end long enough to form a clasp with the glass button, make an Overhand Knot.

2. Slide a bead onto one strand of the ribbon and make one Overhand Knot in both ribbon strands; slide a bead onto the other strand and make one Overhand Knot in both ribbon strands. Repeat this pattern for the length of your bracelet.

3. Tie one final knot in the end and trim the ribbon ends.

4. Wrap the knot with embroidery floss and attach your glass button.

change it up

The variations between the different strands of this necklace make it one of my favorites. To make the first section, tie Square Knots in one set of novelty fibers. Add another set of novelty fibers to the first by tying two Placement Knots at intervals. For the third section, use the Twist & Shout technique, then tie it to the second set and wrap the ends.

instructions:

1. String seed beads onto jewelry wire and finish the ends with crimp beads.

2. Follow instructions for Wrapping with Alternating Colors to wrap a thick core fiber with two colors of floss.

3. Follow instructions for Wrapping with Alternating Colors to wrap a thin core with four colors of novelty fibers.

4. Finish the fiber strands with fiber crimps.

5. Attach one end of all three strands to a large jump ring. Repeat for the other end of the strands.

6. Attach the clasp and pendant.

materials

embroidery floss (2 colors), core fibers (1 thick, 1 thin), novelty fibers (4 colors), clasp, fiber crimps, jewelry wire, large jump rings, pendant, seed beads, tube crimp beads

orange blossom

For this simple yet charming bracelet, create two Twist & Shout strands using blue cord. Clamp both ends with fiber crimps, stitch on a fabric flower, and attach a clasp to finish.

45

materials

embroidery floss (3 colors), clasp, fiber crimps, jump rings, 3 glass beads

instructions:

1. Cut one strand of each color floss (for three strands total) four times the desired length of the bracelet, plus extra for finishing. Knot them together at one end.

2. Use one strand to tie an Overhand Knot over the other two strands. Repeat using Strand #2, then repeat using Strand #3. Continue this pattern for the length of the bracelet. (Note: Each color should be visible every third knot.)

3. Finish the ends with fiber crimps.

4. Slide beads onto the knotted piece.

5. Attach the jump rings and clasp.

rock & roll

A 4-Strand Weave produces a round braid with a rich texture, apparent even when you use one color thread. An eye-catching silver clasp takes the black leather used for this 4-Strand Weave bracelet upscale.

instructions:

1. Cut four strands of floss eight times the length of the finished bracelet, plus extra for finishing. Fold them in half, tie a knot in the middle about 1" from the loop, and pin the knot to the knotting board. Now you will have eight strands.

2. Divide the eight strands into two groups of four. With the group on the left, follow the instructions for the Basic Diagonal Stripe pattern for about 2". Repeat with the strands on the right.

3. Redivide your strands into three groups, with two strands on each side and four strands in the middle.

4. Tie Overhand Knots on both outside groups for about 2".

5. Tie Square Knots with the middle strands until you come even with the Overhand Knot strands.

6. Combine all the strands and complete Square Knots for approximately 3".

7. Repeat steps #3, #4, #5, and #2, in that order.

8. Attach fiber crimps and a clasp.

9. Stitch on the velvet flowers to finish.

materials

embroidery floss (variegated), clasp, fiber crimps, needle and thread, velvet flowers

copper beauties

Alternating Placement Knots with beads makes a simple, but striking, bracelet. To create a matching necklace, simply lengthen the fibers, create longer knotted segments, and add a treasured pin as a pendant.

This sweet little bracelet uses three colors of floss tied in a Diagonal Stripe Pattern for one half of the bracelet. The miniature glass bottle is filled with "fairy dust" to help all of your dreams come true.

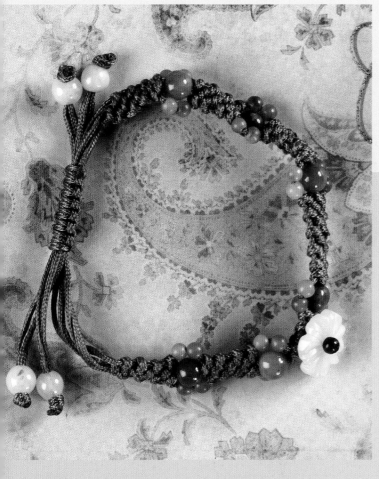

forest flower

A bracelet made of woven cord worked into a Diagonal Stripe Pattern with beads gets an unusual closure. The ends are overlapped and then covered with a separate piece of cord that is tied in a series of Square Knots. This allows the ends to be tightened or loosened as needed.

From a private collection.

49

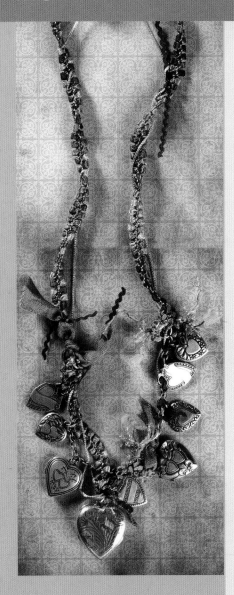

memento necklace

This necklace was a gift from my daughter. She created this piece by taking my favorite silver heart bracelet, attaching a necklace chain to each end, and weaving novelty threads through the bracelet and around the chain. At intervals she tied snippets of novelty threads into knots. Each of these heart lockets holds a picture of my children or my grandchildren. I love this piece!

materials

metallic thread (copper, copper/black, copper/silver), beads, clasps, jewelry wire

instructions:

Here are three different techniques for making pretty copper bracelets that coordinate beautifully.

bracelet 1:

1. Cut four threads and one length of wire; knot them together.

2. Make a series of Square Knots, using two strands of the metallic thread plus the wire as the core strand. As you go along, randomly add one or more beads to the wire, tying Square Knots below the beads to hold them in place.

3. Continue knotting to the end of your bracelet. Knot the loose ends, attach your clasp with wire, and trim the wire and metallic strands.

bracelet 2:

1. Cut three metallic strands and one length of wire; knot them together.

2. Make a series of Overhand Knots using two strands of metallic thread plus the wire as the core strand.

3. As you go along, randomly add a bead or beads to your wire and tie Overhand Knots below the beads to hold them in place.

4. Continue knotting to the end of your bracelet. Knot the loose ends, attach your clasp with wire, and trim the wire and metallic strands.

bracelet 3:

1. Measure two threads of copper/silver, one thread of copper/black, and one length of wire; knot them together.

2. Make a series of Square Knots using copper/black thread and wire as the core. Add a bead and tie a Square Knot under the bead. Tie a second series of Square Knots.

3. Pull the two copper/silver threads to the side and tie a series of Overhand Knots down the middle, using the wire as the core strand and tying with the copper/black thread.

4. Pull the two outside copper/silver threads down the side of the Overhand Knots and tie a Square Knot. Continue this series as desired. Continue as in step 2.

5. Knot the loose ends, attach your clasp with wire, and trim the wire and metallic strands.

materials

embroidery floss (4 colors), beads, clasp, decorative pin, jewelry wire

instructions

1. Cut one strand of wire and one strand of each color floss four times the desired length plus extra for beading and finishing. Knot them together at one end.

2. Following the instructions for the Basic Diagonal Stripe pattern, create a section as long as desired. Add beads to the wire, pull the loose threads down behind the beads, and begin the Diagonal Stripe pattern again. Repeat as desired.

3. Attach a clasp and trim the thread ends.

4. Embellish with the decorative pin. (Note: Whenever you want a different look for this piece, just replace the pin with another.)

free-for-all

The great thing about a project like this that it really lets you be creative. To start, tie together coordinating fibers with a large knot in the middle and stitch or glue a special button over the knot. Next comes the fun part: knot, bead, or do as your whim dictates to each individual strand. There's no pattern, no right or wrong—just whatever you want to do!

instructions:

1. To create the first strand, cut a piece of wire the length of a bracelet plus extra for finishing the ends. String beads onto the wire and attach the ends through one set of holes on the multi-strand clasp.

2. To create the second strand, repeat step 1.

3. To create the third strand, use four strands of novelty fibers about eight times the length of the finished bracelet. (Note: The length of the strands will vary depending on the width of the fibers.) Follow the instructions for a 4-Strand Weave. Attach the completed strand to the clasp.

4. To create the fourth strand, cut three strands of novelty fibers about three times the length of the finished bracelet. (Note: The length of the strands will vary depending on the width of the fibers.) Tie one loose Overhand Knot in the end and follow the instructions for 1-2-3 Weaving for the length of the bracelet. Knot the loose end and attach the completed strand to the clasp.

5. To create the fifth strand, cut four strands of novelty fibers about four times the length of the finished bracelet. (Note: The length of the strands will vary depending on the width of the fibers.) Create a series of square knots for the entire length. Attach the completed strand to the clasp to finish.

materials

novelty fibers, jewelry wire, multi-strand clasp, seed beads

For this sparkly gemstone bracelet, tie blue embroidery floss to one cabochon, make several Square Knots, and tie the other end of the strand to the next cabochon. Repeat this process until all the jewels are connected. Add a dot of glue on each knot finish with a clasp.

back in black

Alternating woven sections with beads and finishing with a high-quality clasp makes this bracelet Black Tie dressy or Casual Friday cool.

54

To create this sparkler, use large jump rings to connect rhinestone rings. Then cut four strands of novelty threads, fold them in half, and tie them onto a rhinestone ring. Tie Square Knots for about one quarter of the desired length of your bracelet. Repeat to create the other side. To make a matching necklace, simply use longer threads and additional rhinestone rings.

easy shimmer

This bracelet is made of metallic cord tied in a Diagonal Stripe Pattern. The cord is looped over the ends of the rhinestone chain before knotting. It's simply tied onto the wrist with a knot.

55

naturally vintage necklace

materials

embroidery floss, **pearl cotton**, **soft silk ribbon**, beads, crimp beads, jewelry wire, lace, large vintage button, needle and thread, vintage-looking quilt pieces

instructions:

1. To create one section of the necklace, cut several short segments of embroidery floss and tie them into Overhand or Square Knots. (Note: To create more texture and interest, vary the tightness of the knots and the number of floss strands you use for each segment.) Tie or stitch the knotted segments to lace and quilt pieces to create a "chain" about one-fifth the desired length of the necklace. Repeat to create a second "chain."

2. Stitch the end of a length of ribbon to the back of the lace or quilt piece at the end of one of the "chains" created in step 1. Thread the ribbon through a large vintage button and stitch the loose end to the back of the lace or quilt piece at the end of the second "chain." Set aside the section.

3. Cut a piece of wire half the desired length of the necklace, plus extra for knotting, beading, and finishing. Thread beads onto the wire for about two-fifths the length of the necklace. Add a crimp bead to one end and crimp it.

4. To secure the other end of the beaded section, tie three strands of pearl cotton to the wire at the point where the beads end. Using the wire as one strand, follow the instructions for the Square Knots with Raised Picot technique to create a short, knotted segment. Separate the wire from the pearl cotton, add a bead, and then repeat the Square Knot with Raised Picot pattern. Tie a knot at the end of the segment.

5. Stitch or tie one end of the section created in steps 1 and 2 to one end of the section created in steps 3 and 4. Stitch or tie the loose ends together to finish.

naturally vintage bracelet

A matching bracelet, or set of bracelets, can be created by simply making the vintage necklace shorter.

instructions:

1. Thread a large brass bead onto one color of cotton ribbon and tie an Overhand Knot on either side of the bead.

2. Using six Square Knots, tie two strands of the second color of thread to the first section about 2" from the bead. Still working with the second color, tie an Overhand Knot, add a bead, and tie a second Overhand Knot. Attach the end of this section to the back of the tin piece.

3. Attach a clasp to both ends of the bracelet. For the ribbon end, attach the clasp by wrapping wire around both the clasp and the knotted sections. On the remaining end, attach the clasp with a jump ring.

materials

cotton ribbons (2 colors), brass-colored tin piece, clasp, jewelry wire, jump ring, large brass beads

round and round

Gold and aqua fibers are combined with vintage brass rings and beaded wire for this necklace. To create, tie brass rings together with fiber strands and beaded lengths of wire. Use a variety of knots and patterns on the fibers.

it's a wrap

materials

leather cord, beads, clasp, jewelry wire

instructions:

1. Cut a leather cord so that it is long enough to wrap around your arm several times; also cut a variety of different lengths of wire.

2. Wrap one length of wire around your cord several times until it is secure. Add as many beads to the wire as desired. Wrap the remainder of the wire around your cord to secure the beads.

3. Repeat step 2 at different intervals on the leather cord.

4. To attach the clasp, wrap more wire around the cord and the clasp.

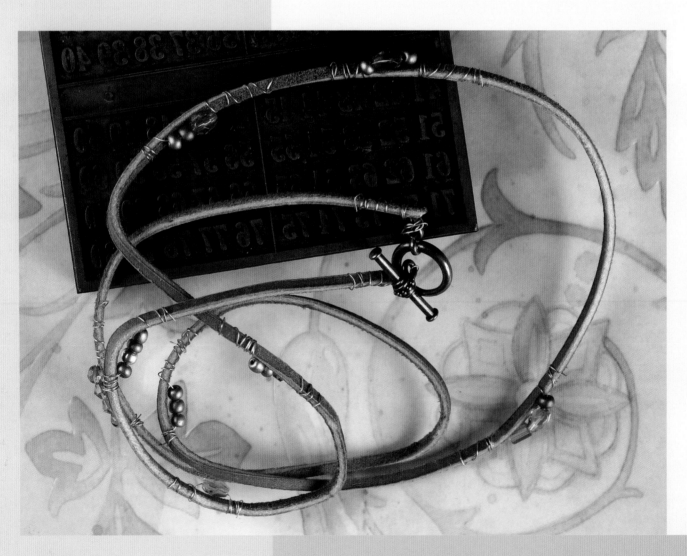

instructions:

1. Measure ten strands of novelty fibers and one strand of wire to eight times the desired length of the bracelet, plus extra for finishing. Combine all of the strands and fold them in half. Tie a knot about ½" from the looped end.

2. Weave the strands in a Chevron Pattern to the middle of the bracelet. (Note: Carry the wire with one of the novelty fiber strands.)

3. Divide the fiber strands into two groups, leaving the wire free. Wrap one group of fibers with one thin fiber.

4. String beads on the wire down the middle as far as desired.

5. Weave all strands (including the wire) in a Chevron Pattern for the rest of the bracelet's length. Knot the end and attach your clasp.

materials

various novelty fibers, beads, jewelry wire, novelty clasp

seasonal delight

materials

novelty fibers and ribbons, charm, clasp, jump ring, needle and thread, pendant, ribbon crimps

instructions:

1. Cut several novelty fibers two to three times the desired length of the necklace, plus extra for finishing. Fold them in half and tie them together in a knot 2" from the looped end.

2. Divide the fibers into eight to ten groups of one to four strands each. For each group, tie different knots in various patterns, such as a series of Square Knots alternated with Overhand Knots or Braiding and Weaving 1-2-3 interspersed with Overhand Knots. (Note: One pair of fiber groups on the necklace shown uses a single beaded ribbon.)

3. Attach large ribbon crimps to the loose ends of each group. Attach the ribbon crimps to the clasp.

4. Use a jump ring to attach a charm to your pendant, and then stitch your pendant to the center knot to finish.

brass rings

This piece uses the Twist & Shout techniques and Overhand Knots to showcase brass rings and a pendant. Simple, but stunning.

From a private collection.

This necklace has an organic texture, thanks to a variety of beads and the loose, flowing look of the fiber sections. It started as a ready-made piece purchased on sale from a major high-end clothing store. To make it unique, I wrapped brown fibers around the chain, knotting them at intervals, and left the thread ends hanging. With some outfits, I pin a warrior doll to it for extra good luck.

61

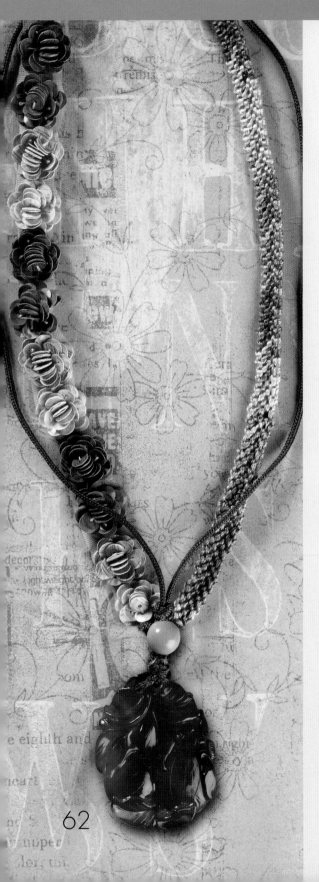

materials

cord, embroidery floss, sequin flower trim, bead, clasp, needle and thread, pendant, ribbon crimps

instructions:

1. Cut a piece of cord the length of the necklace plus extra for knotting and finishing. Attach the pendant to the center of the cord and tie a knot. Add a bead and tie another knot.

2. To create the first side of the necklace, cut your trim to half the desired length of the necklace. Stitch one end of the trim to the back of the first knot created in step 1.

3. To create the second side of the necklace, cut six strands of embroidery floss four times the desired length of the section, plus extra for finishing. Tie them together with a knot 1" from the end. Follow the instructions for a Chevron pattern until you match the length of the first side of the necklace, and then tie a knot. Trim the loose ends close to the knots on both ends. Seal the ends with a little glue. When dry, stitch one end of the Chevron strand to the back of the first knot created in step 1.

4. Attach ribbon ends to both ends of the necklace and attach your clasp to finish.

knotted

warrior

This warrior figure is a good-luck piece. I have a wonderful series of bead warriors and women that hang on my wall on a vintage hat rack when I am not wearing them. The simple knot closure makes this piece particularly interesting.

From a private collection.

materials

silk seam-binding cord (one thick, one thin), charms, clasp, jump ring, ribbon ends, vintage beaded necklace, vintage pocket watch

instructions:

1. Open the back of the watch, remove the gears, and insert your charms. Close the watch.

2. Take two strands of seam binding cord (one thick, one thin) and fold them in half. Tie the looped ends to the loop on the watch.

3. Using the thick cord as a core strand and the thin cord as the knotting strand, tie Overhand Knots along one side of the necklace for as long as desired. Repeat on the other side, and then finish the loose ends with ribbon ends.

4. Attach the vintage beaded necklace to the watch loop.

5. Cut a length of thin cord about 1½ times the length of the necklace. Thread the cord through a loop at the center of the beaded necklace and tie a knot. Wrap one half of the cord around one side of the beaded necklace. Attach a ribbon end to the unwrapped strand and the thick, knotted cord. Repeat for the other side of the necklace.

6. Attach the beaded necklace and ribbon ends to the clasp.

memories made

Create this necklace by beading crystal beads on a thin wire. Tie Overhand Knots with variegated floss adding small beads at random. Connect the beaded and knotted lengths to a small copper jewelry frame and wear on days when memories seem most important.

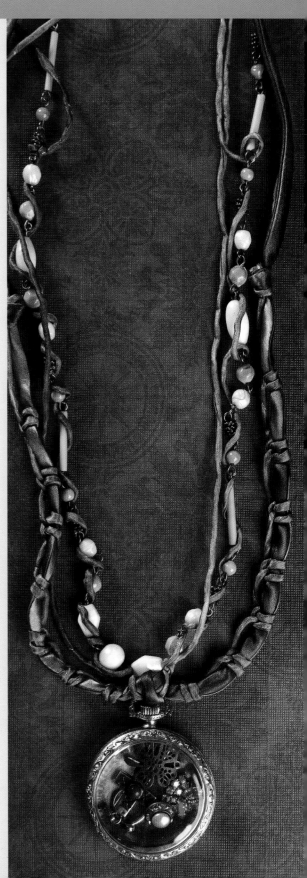

index